EYE TO EYE

HOW
ANIMALS
SEE
THE
WORLD

◉

STEVE JENKINS

Houghton Mifflin Harcourt • Boston New York

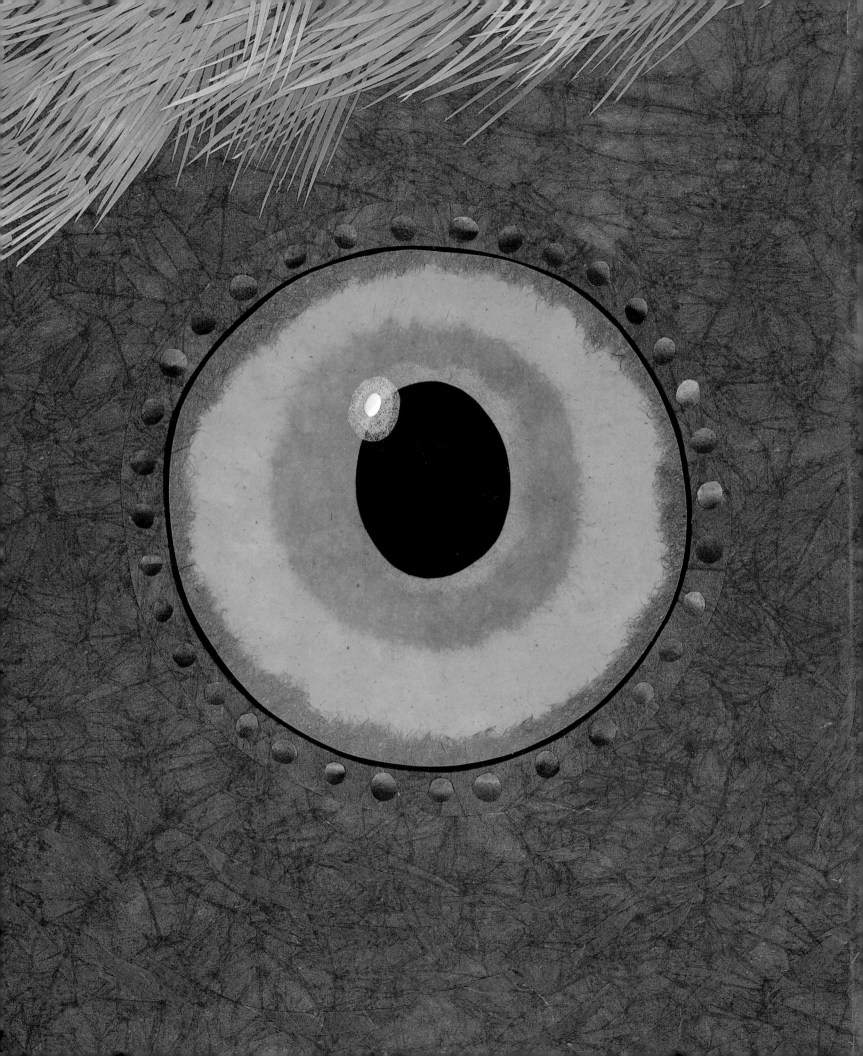

ost animals rely on their vision, more than any other sense, to find out what is going on around them. For these creatures, the eyes are the most important link to the world.

Being able to see helps animals communicate, find food, avoid predators, or locate a mate. Animals are found in just about every habitat on earth—from deep oceans to snow-covered mountains—and they have developed extraordinarily diverse eyes and ways of using them. Some creatures can do no more than tell day from night, while others can see colors invisible to humans, spot prey at a great distance, or find their way in what appears to us to be total darkness.

So turn the page and meet animals with more than 100 eyeballs, eyes that can look in two directions at the same time, eyeballs the size of a basketball, and many more.

The **red-crowned Amazon parrot** (*left*) has excellent color vision, useful for finding the fruit and flowers it feeds on. The **jumping stick insect** (*right*) is actually a kind of grasshopper. Its protruding eyes allow it to see in many directions at once.

The first eyes

There could be no life on earth without the sun. Since the planet's earliest days, the sun has warmed it and bathed it in light. The first forms of life, tiny organisms adrift in the oceans, depended on this heat and light. Like modern-day plants, they absorbed sunlight and used it to produce their food. But for more than three billion years, all living things were blind. They sensed only what they could touch, taste, or feel. Then, about 600 million years ago, a few animals—the ancestors of modern jellyfish and sponges—acquired an important new ability. They had become the first animals that could see. Their eyes were just simple clusters of light-

Four kinds of eye

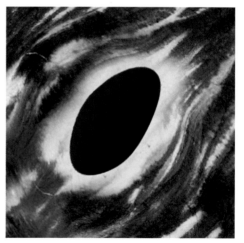

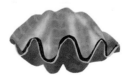

The simplest eye is a cluster of light-sensitive cells known as an **eyespot**. This eye can't form images, but it does detect light. Some worms have eyespots, as do starfish, which have an eyespot at the tip of each leg.

A giant clam has thousands of **pinhole eyes**. In each, a small opening focuses light as it enters the eye. Pinhole eyes can form detailed images. They don't admit much light, however, so the images are dimmer than those created by a compound or camera eye.

sensitive cells, but they gave these animals a big advantage. The shadow of a predator could send them moving to safety, while creatures that couldn't see at all were more likely to be eaten.

Millions of years passed and eyes continued to evolve. Highly developed visual systems appeared, many that could discern colors or produce sharp images. Eyes and ways of seeing became more and more diverse. Today there are dozens of different animal eyes, but most are variations on one of four basic designs.

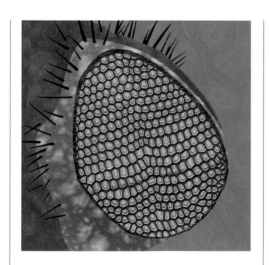

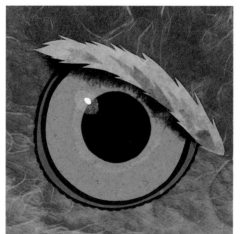

All eyes contain cells called photoreceptors. These cells convert light into signals that are interpreted by an animal's brain. In the camera eye, the photoreceptors are found on the retina.

Dragonflies and other arthropods have **compound eyes**. Each is composed of hundreds or thousands of individual lenses, or facets. In some animals, the facets form separate images. In others, they combine to create a single picture.

The **camera eye** employs a lens to focus light on the sensitive surface of a retina. It is found in all birds, amphibians, reptiles, and mammals, including humans. Octopuses, box jellyfish, and a few other animals also have camera eyes.

Move away from the light.

The eyespots of the **sea slug** can detect light, but they can't form images or perceive the slug's own brilliant colors. This kind of eye has been around for hundreds of millions of years.

First, I'll take a look around.

The eyes of the **garden snail** are perched at the end of two long stalks, so it can look in every direction without sticking its head out of its shell. The snail's eyes can resolve images, but they function mainly as light detectors. Sensing the shadow of a bird or other predator can help the snail survive.

A pinhole eye

Animals much like the **nautilus** have been around for 500 million years. Its pinhole eyes can discern objects and other animals, but only if they are large or very close. These eyes have no lens, so water flows in and out of the nautilus's pupil.

How many eyes?

The **Atlantic bay scallop** is also known as the blue-eyed scallop. Its two rows of blue eyeballs are sensitive to movement as well as light, allowing the scallop to snap shut when danger threatens. The number of eyes can vary—one scallop was found to have 111 eyeballs.

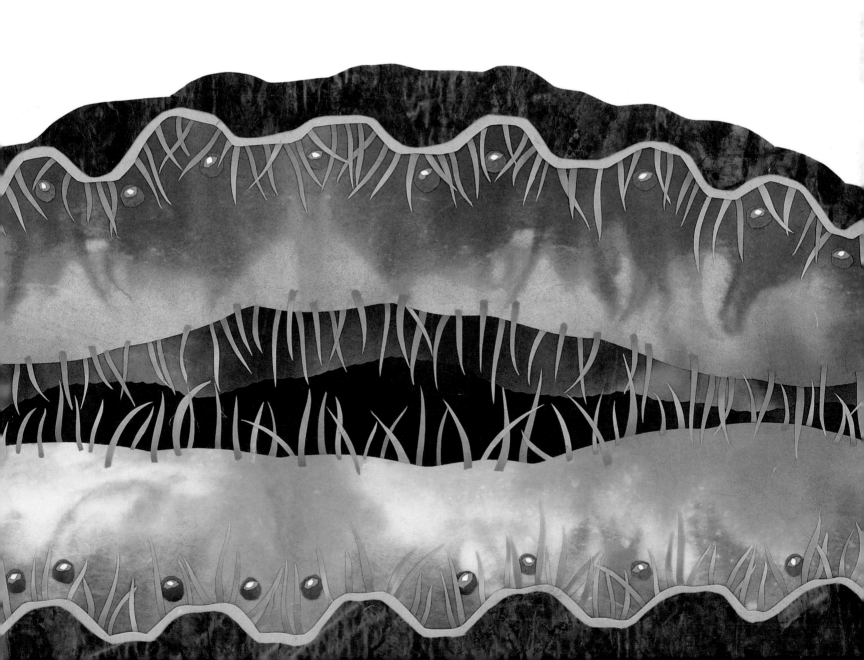

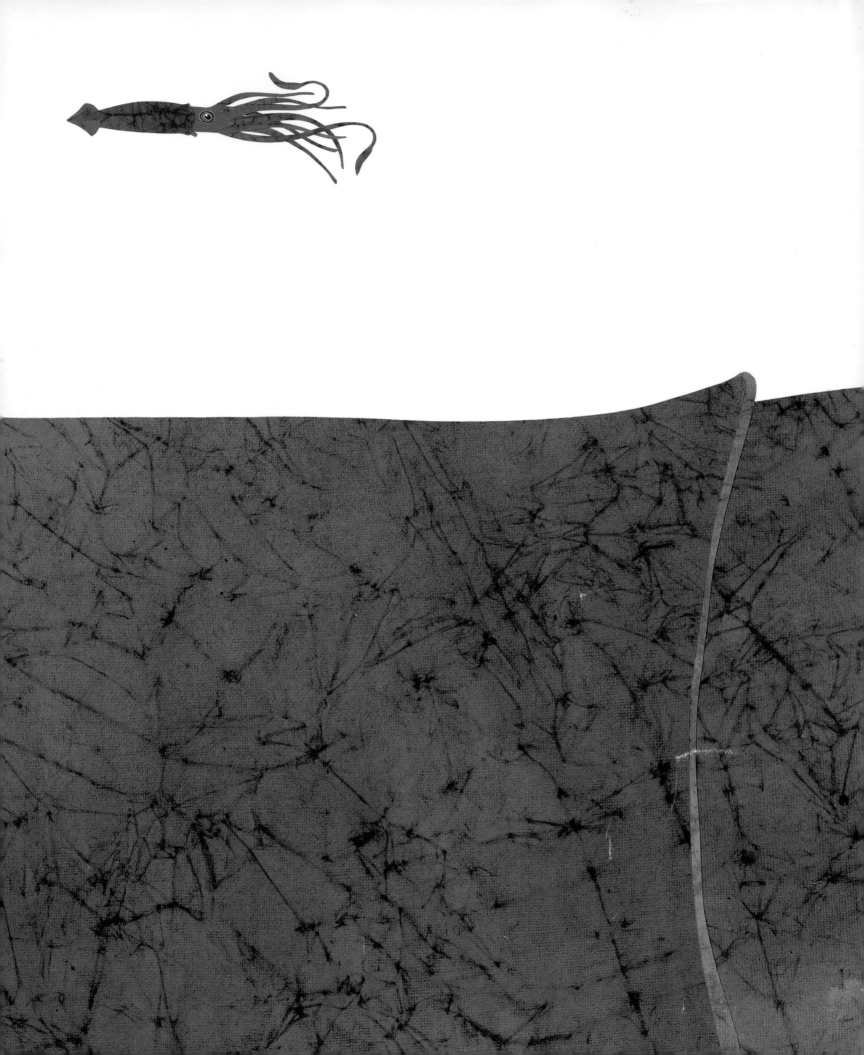

The biggest eye

The eyes of the **colossal squid** are each the size of a basketball—the largest of any animal. The deep ocean waters where this squid lives are completely dark. Its huge eyes, however, can detect the faint glow of tiny bioluminescent creatures when they are disturbed by an approaching sperm whale, the squid's archenemy.

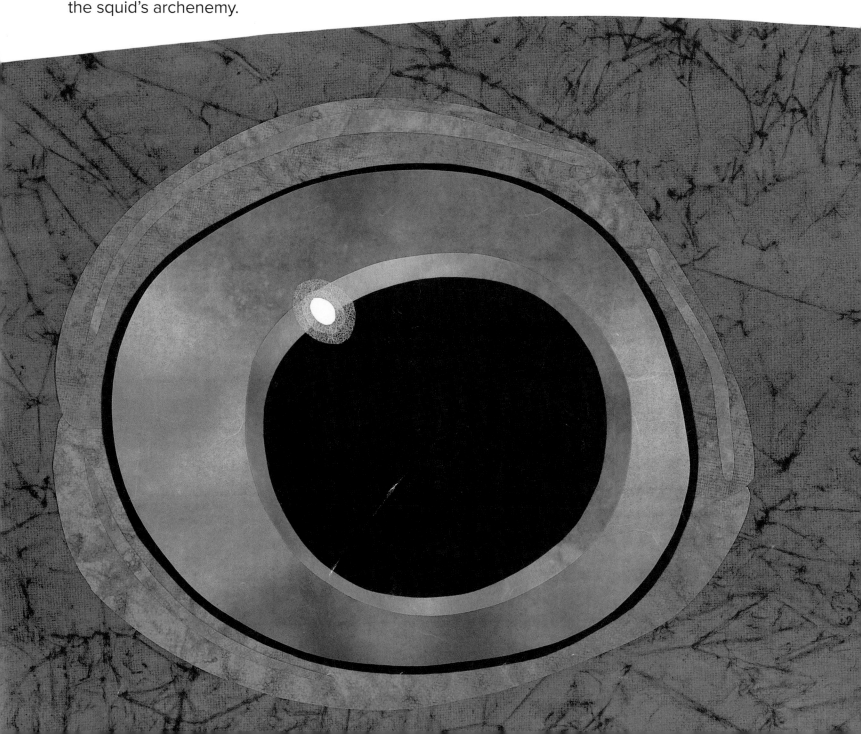

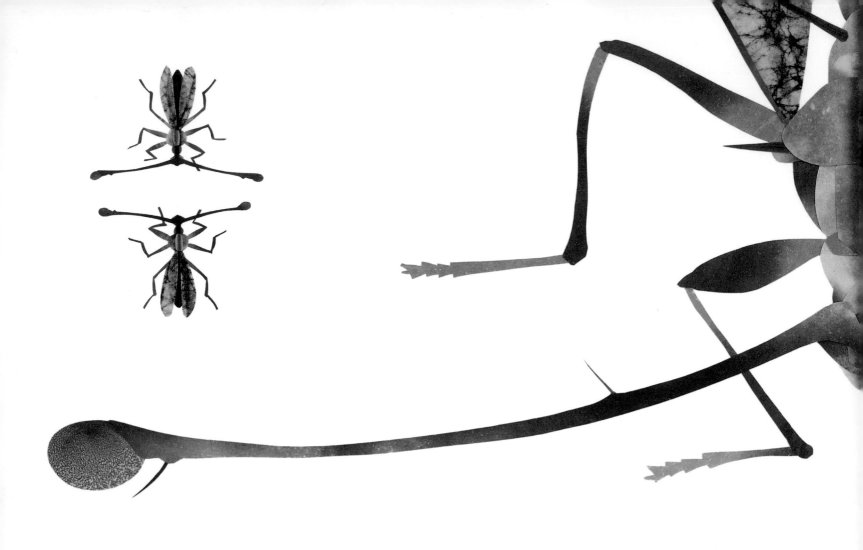

Moving target

The **bullfrog** doesn't appear to see things that aren't moving. It eats insects, but face-to-face with a motionless fly, it will starve to death. The frog's eyes also help it swallow its prey. They press downward through openings in its skull, forcing food down its throat.

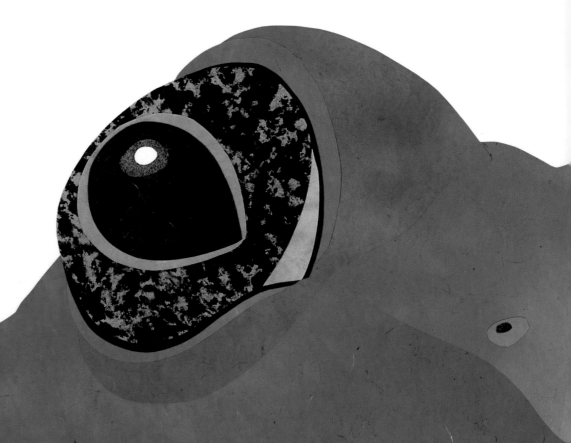

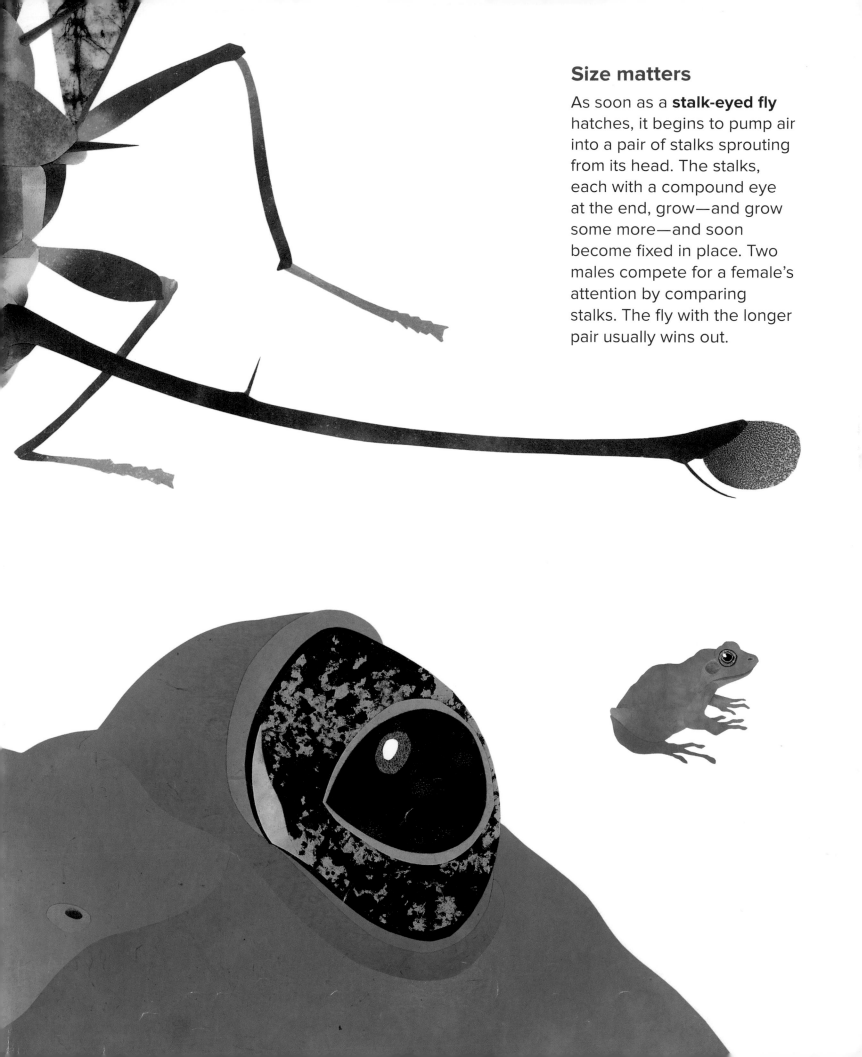

Size matters

As soon as a **stalk-eyed fly** hatches, it begins to pump air into a pair of stalks sprouting from its head. The stalks, each with a compound eye at the end, grow—and grow some more—and soon become fixed in place. Two males compete for a female's attention by comparing stalks. The fly with the longer pair usually wins out.

Seeing the invisible

The **blue mountain swallowtail butterfly** can see most of the colors that we see, as well as some that we can't. Its compound eyes are sensitive to ultraviolet light —high-frequency light that is invisible to us. Many flowers attract butterflies by displaying stripes and patterns visible only in ultraviolet light. This insect's eyes also provide a wide field of vision, allowing it to see in nearly a full circle.

You're getting warmer.

A pair of heat-sensing organs on the face of the **green pit viper** can "see" the body heat of a bird or mammal. Radiant heat, or infrared radiation, is really just a kind of light that humans can't see. These organs, or pits, are not eyes in the normal sense, but with them the snake can form an image of its warm-blooded prey in what we would perceive as complete darkness.

If looks could kill . . .

The **jumping spider** is a hunter, and it relies on its eight eyes to find and kill its prey. It has two pairs of eyes on each side of its head (not visible in this view) that detect movement. A wide-set pair of eyes on the front of its head provide depth perception. And the two large eyes in the middle of its face form detailed images, giving it the keenest vision of any spider.

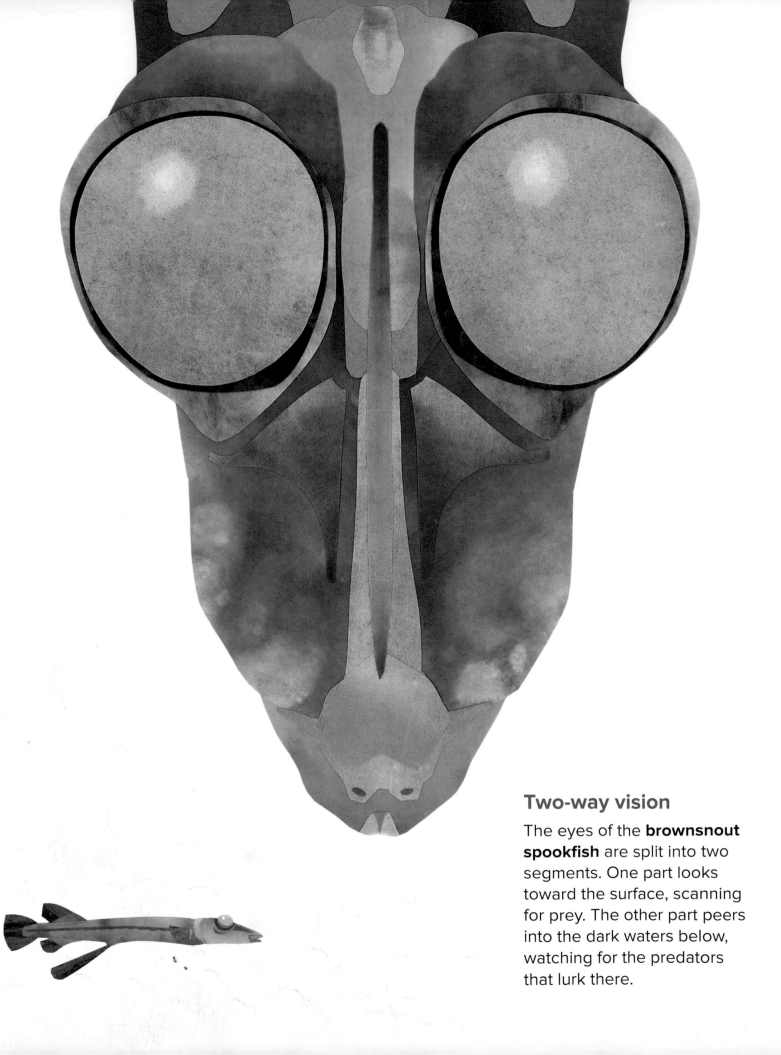

Two-way vision

The eyes of the **brownsnout spookfish** are split into two segments. One part looks toward the surface, scanning for prey. The other part peers into the dark waters below, watching for the predators that lurk there.

Two plus one

The **tuatara**, the last surviving member of an ancient family of reptiles, has a third eye on the top of its head. This eye is sensitive to light, but it cannot form images.

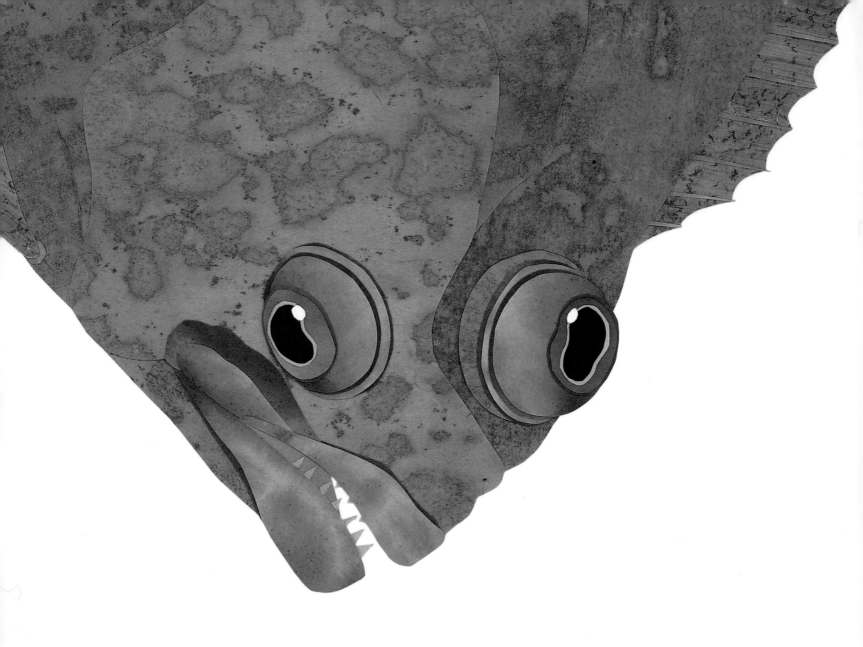

Things are looking up.

A young **halibut**, like most fish, has an eye on each side of its body. As it gets older, however, one eye migrates over the top of the fish's head. Eventually, both eyes end up on the same side. The halibut spends most of its adult life lying on its side on the bottom of the ocean, and this arrangement means that both eyes will be directed upward, away from the sea floor.

Over, under, sideways, down

The **panther chameleon** can move and focus its eyes independently. It can look in two directions at once, watching for prey and danger at the same time.

360 degrees

The compound eyes of the **ghost crab** are positioned on stalks that swivel. The eyesight of this crab is so sharp that it can spot and track a flying insect, then snatch it out of the air. It can also watch for danger approaching from any side.

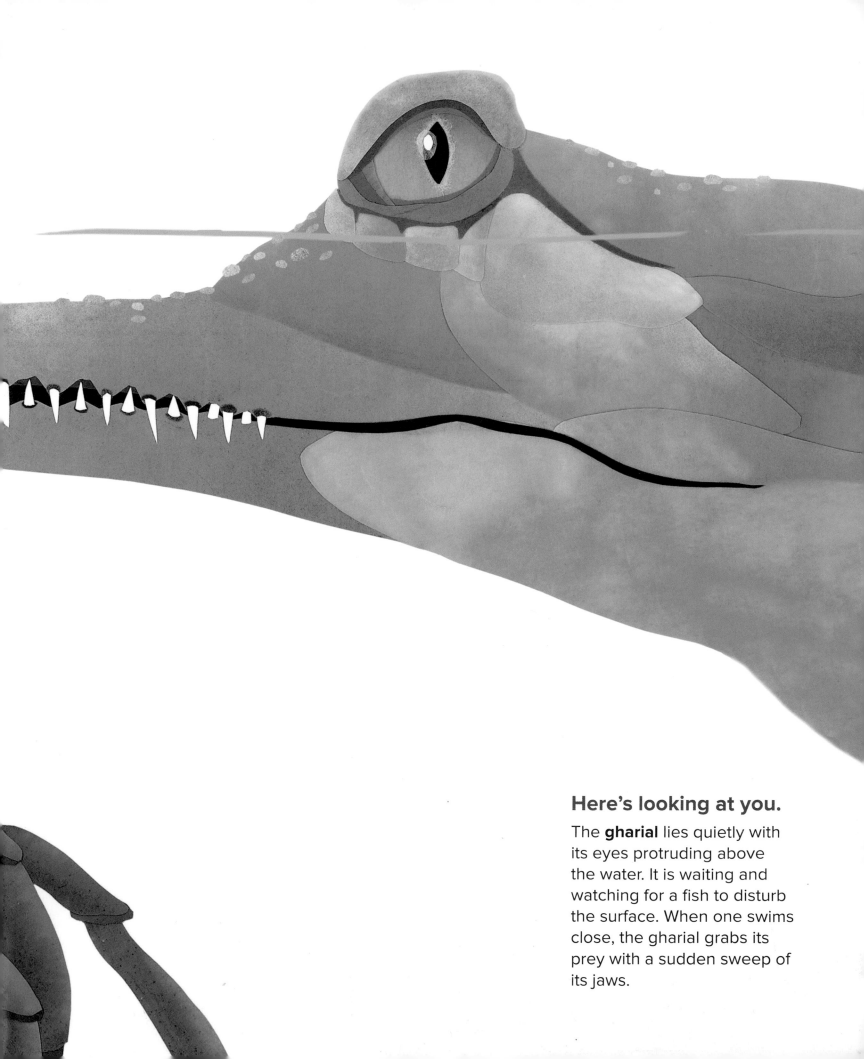

Here's looking at you.

The **gharial** lies quietly with its eyes protruding above the water. It is waiting and watching for a fish to disturb the surface. When one swims close, the gharial grabs its prey with a sudden sweep of its jaws.

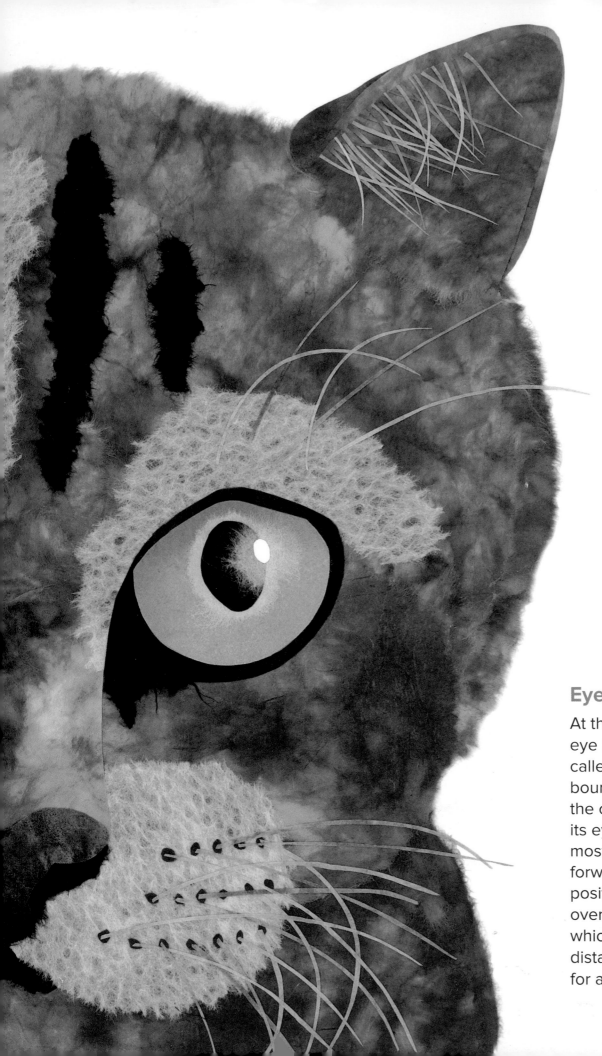

Eyes of a hunter

At the back of the **housecat**'s eye is a reflective layer called a tapetum. This layer bounces light back through the cat's retina, improving its eyesight in dim light. Like most predators, cats also have forward-facing eyes. This position gives the two eyes overlapping fields of vision, which makes it easier to judge distance—an important ability for a hunter.

Built-in goggles

The **hippopotamus** spends much of its time in lakes and rivers. It can see well underwater, where its eyes are protected by a special clear membrane. Like most herbivores, the hippo has eyes positioned on either side of its head. This gives it a wide field of view to watch for lions and other predators.

Zip it

The **leopard gecko** is nocturnal, and it can see well in dim light. If this lizard ventures out during the day, its pupils contract to zipper-shaped slits to protect its sensitive eyes against the bright light of the sun.

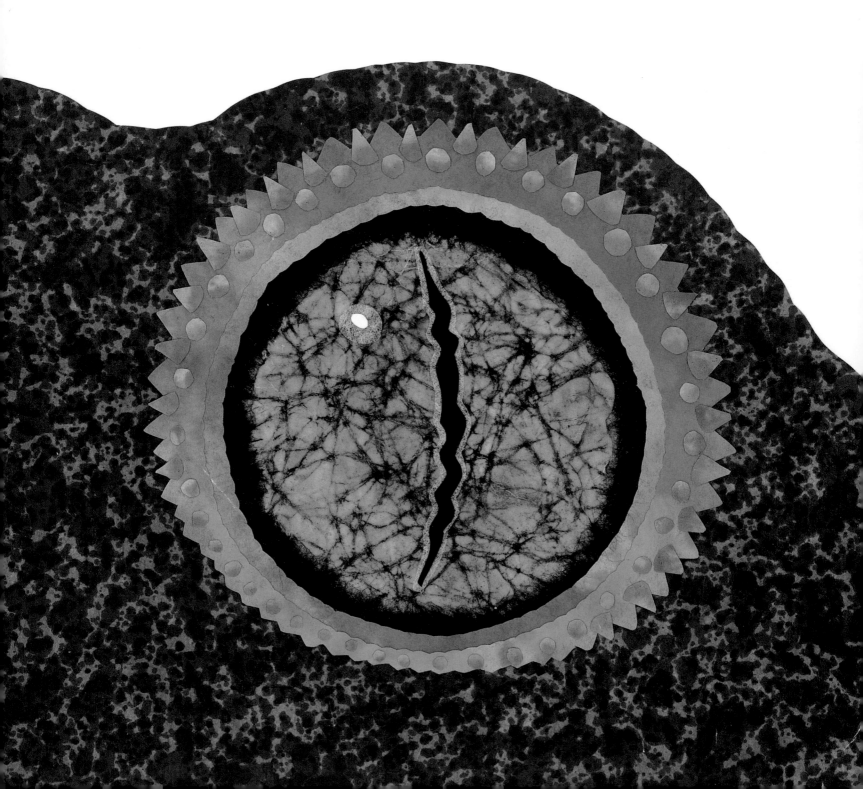

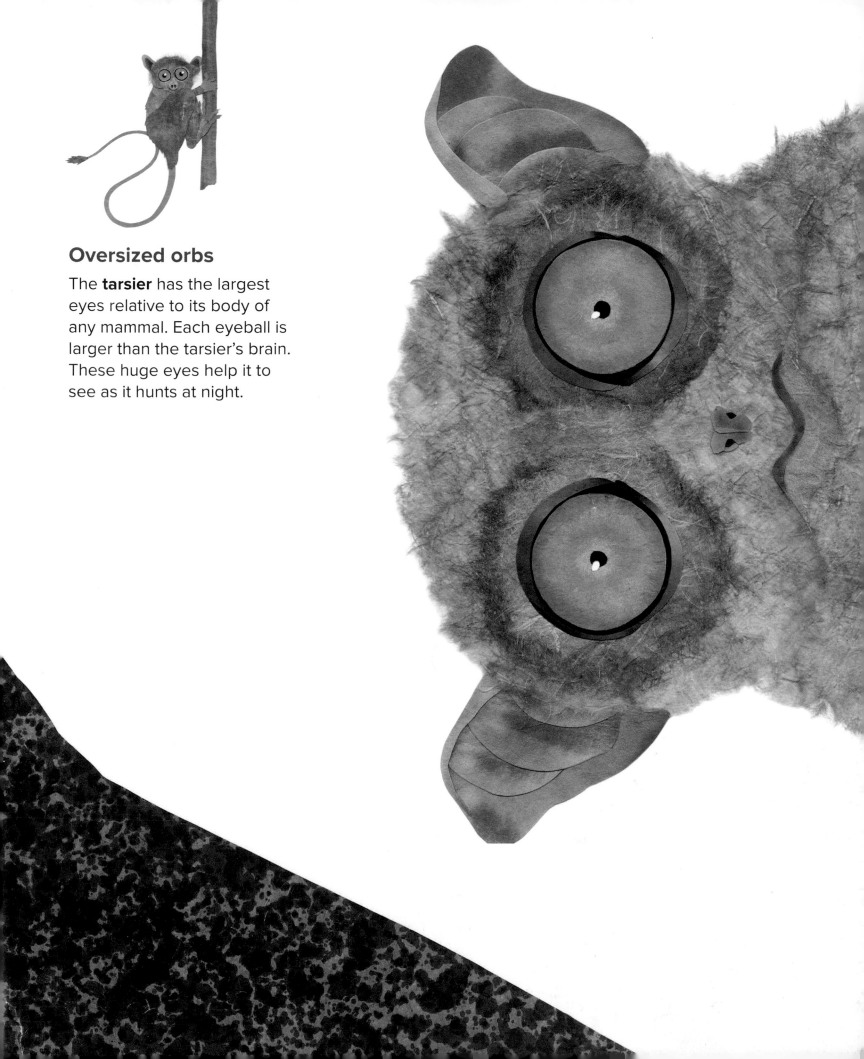

Oversized orbs

The **tarsier** has the largest eyes relative to its body of any mammal. Each eyeball is larger than the tarsier's brain. These huge eyes help it to see as it hunts at night.

Rainbow vision

The eyes of the **mantis shrimp** are the most highly developed in the animal kingdom. They are much more sensitive to color than our own eyes, and they can detect light that is invisible to most other creatures. These eyes help the mantis shrimp find prey and avoid danger in the colorful coral reef habitat where it lives.

Sharp-eyed hunter

The **Eurasian buzzard** has the sharpest eyesight of any animal. Its vision is eight times more accurate than ours — keen enough to home in on a rabbit two miles (3 kilometers) away.

The evolution of the eye

The evolutionary steps from a simple eyespot to a sophisticated camera eye can be seen in animals alive today.

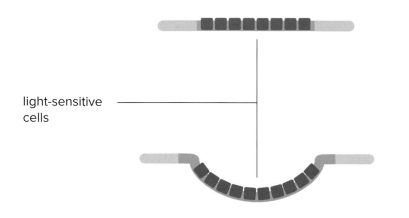

light-sensitive cells

The earliest animal eye was an **eyespot**, a thin layer of light-sensitive cells. This kind of eye, still found in some simple animals, can only distinguish light from dark.

starfish

In the **eyecup**, the layer of light-sensitive cells has become depressed. Light shining on this eye (from any direction other than directly in front) is brighter on one side of the cup, enabling an animal to tell from what direction the light is coming.

hagfish

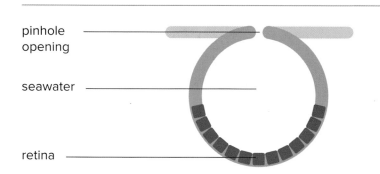

pinhole opening

seawater

retina

In the **pinhole** eye, the cup has almost closed. As in a pinhole camera, a small opening focuses the light entering the eye and forms an image.

nautilus

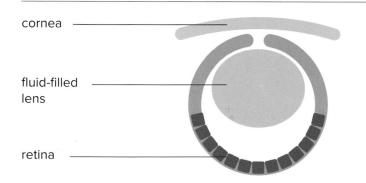

cornea

fluid-filled lens

retina

The **primitive lens eye** contains a fluid-filled pouch that focuses light. The eye is covered by a thin layer of translucent tissue—a cornea.

sea snail

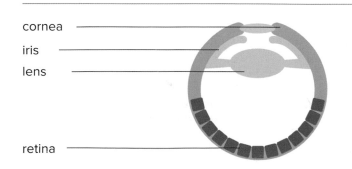

cornea

iris

lens

retina

The **camera eye** includes a transparent cornea and a hard lens that can change shape or position to focus on subjects at different distances.

dog

Animal facts

 red-crowned Amazon parrot
Length: 13 inches (33 centimeters)
Habitat: northeastern Mexico, Florida, California, and Texas
Diet: seeds, fruit, and flowers

 jumping stick insect
Length: 3 inches (76 centimeters)
Habitat: central and western South America
Diet: leaves of tress and shrubs

 sea slug
Length: 2½ inches (6½ centimeters)
Habitat: the Caribbean and Atlantic coastal waters of Europe
Diet: sea anemones

 garden snail
Length (shell): up to 1½ inches (38 millimeters)
Habitat: temperate lands worldwide
Diet: plants, including vegetables, grasses, fruit trees, and flowers

 nautilus
Size: 8 inches (20 centimeters) across
Habitat: Indo-Pacific Ocean
Diet: crabs, shrimp, and fish

 Atlantic bay scallop
Length (shell): 1–3 inches (2½–7½ centimeters)
Habitat: coastal waters of eastern North America
Diet: zooplankton (small drifting marine animals)

 colossal squid
Length: up to 46 feet (14 meters)
Habitat: deep oceans around Antarctica
Diet: fish and other squid

 bullfrog
Length: 5 inches (13 centimeters)
Habitat: ponds and marshes of the Americas, Europe, and China
Diet: insects, small reptiles, and frogs

 stalk-eyed fly
Length: up to ½ inch (13 millimeters)
Habitat: Asia and Africa
Diet: fungi and bacteria

 blue mountain swallowtail
Wingspan: 5½ inches (14 centimeters)
Habitat: northeastern Australia, New Guinea
Diet: flowering shrubs and trees

 green pit viper
Length: 24 inches (60 centimeters)
Habitat: forests of Southeast Asia
Diet: birds, lizards, and frogs

 jumping spider
Length: 1/25–7/8 inch (1–22 millimeters)
Habitat: worldwide, except arctic regions
Diet: insects and other spiders

 brownsnout spookfish
Length: 7 inches (18 centimeters)
Habitat: deep waters of the Atlantic and Pacific Oceans
Diet: shrimp and small marine animals

 tuatara
Length: 30 inches (76 centimeters)
Habitat: New Zealand
Diet: frogs, lizards, eggs, and birds

 halibut
Length: up to 8 feet (2½ meters)
Habitat: northern Atlantic and Pacific Oceans
Diet: crabs, shrimp, octopuses, and fish

 panther chameleon
Length: 18 inches (46 centimeters)
Habitat: forests of Madagascar
Diet: insects

 ghost crab
Width (body): 2 inches (5 centimeters)
Habitat: sandy beaches throughout temperate and tropical parts of the world
Diet: clams, crabs, and other small invertebrates

 gharial
Length: 20 feet (6 meters)
Habitat: rivers of northern India and Nepal
Diet: fish, frogs, and crayfish

 housecat
Length: (head/body) 18 inches (46 centimeters)
Habitat: wherever people live
Diet: cat food (meat), birds, and small mammals

 hippopotamus
Weight: up to 3 tons (2,700 kilograms)
Habitat: rivers and lakes in central and southern Africa
Diet: grass and water plants

 leopard gecko
Length: 10 inches (25 centimeters)
Habitat: arid regions of southern Asia
Diet: insects and worms

 tarsier
Length: 6 inches (15 centimeters)
Habitat: southeast Asia
Diet: small reptiles and birds

 mantis shrimp
Length: 12 inches (30 centimeters)
Habitat: shallow tropical and subtropical seas worldwide
Diet: fish, crabs, shrimp, and shellfish

 Eurasian buzzard
Wingspan: 4 feet (122 centimeters)
Habitat: forests in Europe
Diet: small mammals and birds

Bibliography

Animal Eyes.
By Beth Fielding. Earlylight Books, 2011.

Animal Life. By Charlotte Uhlenbroek. Dorling Kindersley, 2008.

Animal Vision.
By George F. Mason. Morrow Junior Books, 1968.

How Animals See.
By Sandra Sinclair. Facts on File Publications, 1985.

How Nature Works.
Edited by Robin Rees et al. Macmillan Publishing Company, 1992.

Supersense.
By John Downer. Henry Holt and Company, 1988.

Glossary

arthropods
A group of animals with jointed limbs and (usually) a hard, segmented covering, but no backbone. This group includes insects, spiders, scorpions, crabs, and shrimp.

bioluminescent
Describes living organisms that can produce their own light.

cornea
A protective transparent covering on the front of the eye. The cornea is curved and helps focus light.

iris
The colored part of the eye. The iris is a thin layer near the front of the eyeball that controls the size of the pupil.

lens
A hard, clear structure in the eyes of humans and many animals. The lens moves or changes shape to focus light on the retina.

membrane
A thin, flexible layer of tissue.

nocturnal
Active at night.

orb
An eye or eyeball.

pupil
The opening through which light enters the eye. In many animals, the size of this opening changes to adjust to different light levels.

receptor cells
In many advanced eyes, there are two kinds of light receptor cells: rods and cones. Rod cells are sensitive to low levels of light but do not differentiate colors. Cone cells are responsible for color vision—each type of cone cell is sensitive to a different color of light. The number of different cone cells in animal eyes varies. Dogs have two types, humans have three, birds and many fish have four kinds of cone cells, and the mantis shrimp has twelve.

retina
The light-sensitive inner lining of the eyeball. The retina is where receptor cells—rods and cones—are found. It converts light into nerve impulses that are interpreted by the brain.

tapetum
A mirrorlike layer at the back of the eye that increases visual sensitivity in low light. It is found in many fish, reptiles, and mammals (but not humans) and is responsible for eyeshine—the glow created when a light is shined into an animal's eyes at night.

360-degree vision
The ability to see in a complete circle.

ultraviolet light
Light with a shorter wavelength and higher energy than the light we can see. Ultraviolet light is responsible for sunburn, and is visible to many insects, fish, birds, and other creatures.

For Jamie, Alec, and Page

www.hmhbooks.com

The text of this book is set in Proxima Nova.

The illustrations are torn and cut paper.

Library of Congress Cataloging-in-Publication Control Number 2013024004.

ISBN 978-0-547-95907-8

Manufactured in China

SCP 10 9 8 7 6 5 4 3 2 1

4500451730